Dedication

**Sink your roots
into the earth.
Revere the life blood
that is present there.**

TREES TALK

Living things talk.
We talk.
Bees talk.

Creatures of the sea talk.

Birds talk, herds talk.

Polar bears and mares talk.

Cats talk, bats talk,
Yes, nocturnal rats talk.
So why should it surprise us
That trees also talk?

talk talk

talk talk

What are they saying?
What do they know?
Though humans are just learning this
Trees have always acted so.

Slowly, surely, we're uncovering
their ways
Here's what we've discovered
By observing their displays.

On the African plains
The first clues were attained
Where the hot summer sun
Keeps ablazing.

The giraffes do not thirst.
Acacia leaves quench their thirst.
They eat hundreds each day
While they're grazing.

If giraffes ate their fill
From this nourishing tree
There'd be no leaves in sight
When they finished.

But the trees are as clever
As the giraffes that they feed.
They spew tannins
So their taste will diminish.

Twenty minutes it takes
To emit this bitter taste.
The giraffes think the leaves
have gone stale.

So they bound off to find
Another tree of its kind
And must amble
Long ways on the trail.

When the next tree's in sight
The giraffe moves in tight.
What a feast he's about to consume.

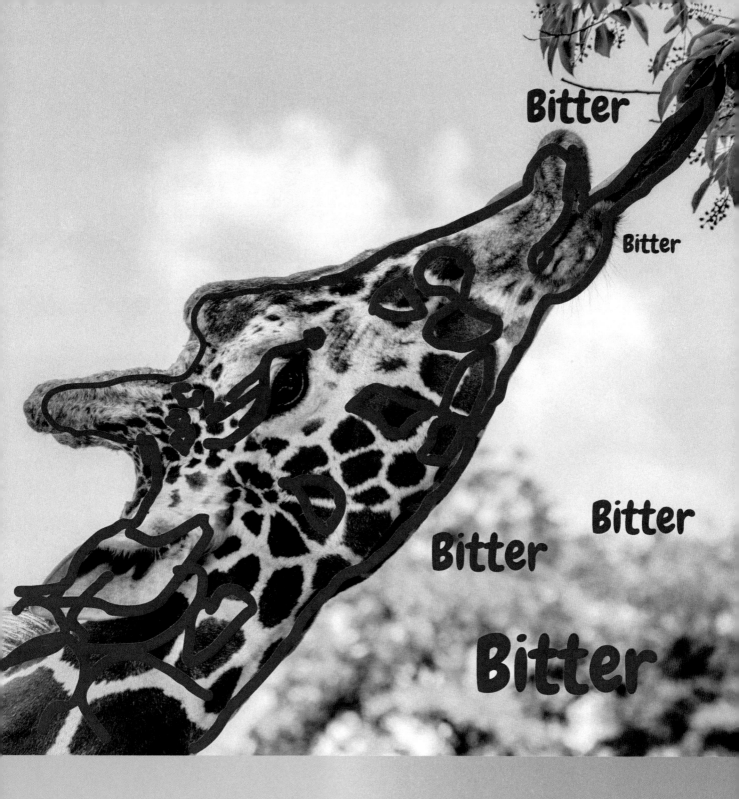

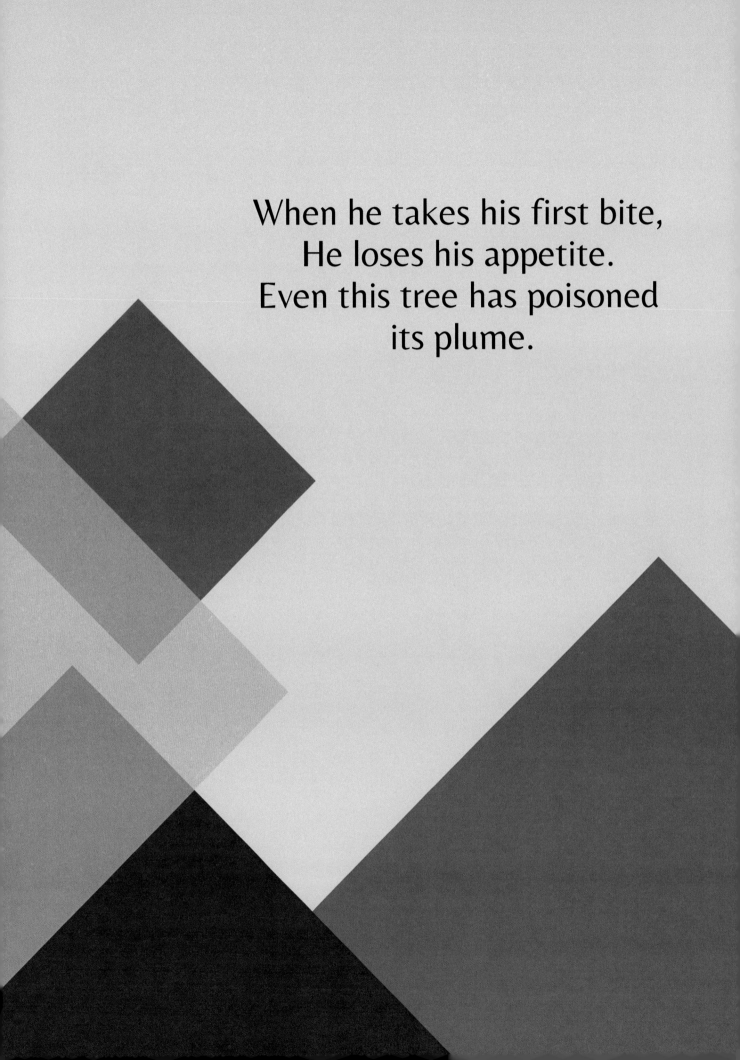

When he takes his first bite,
He loses his appetite.
Even this tree has poisoned
its plume.

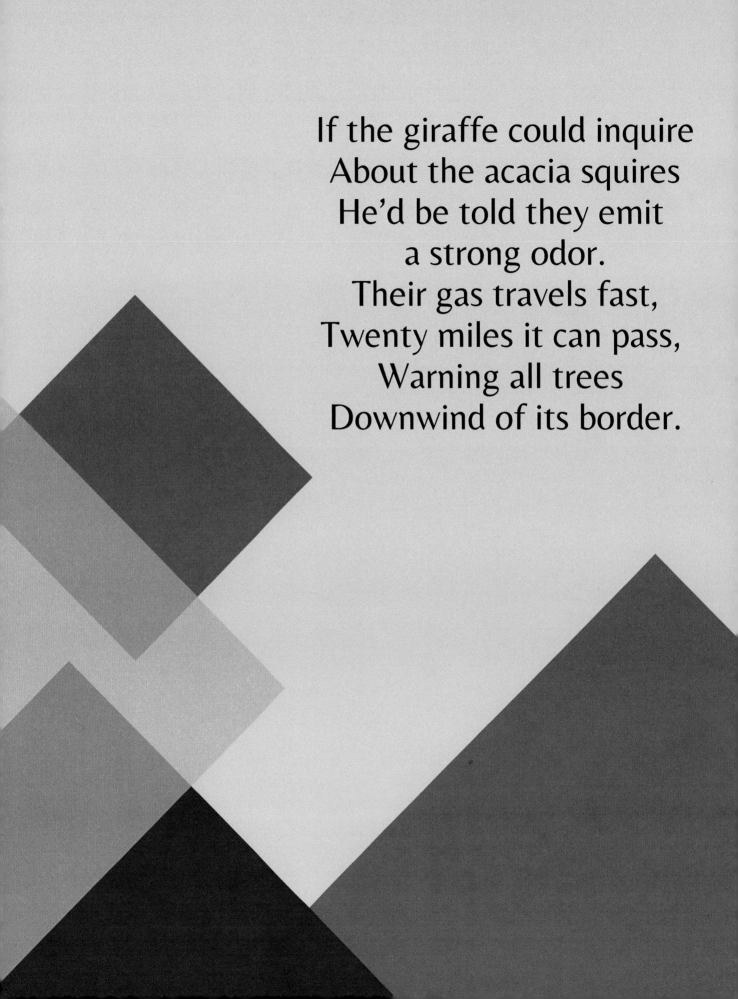

If the giraffe could inquire
About the acacia squires
He'd be told they emit
a strong odor.
Their gas travels fast,
Twenty miles it can pass,
Warning all trees
Downwind of its border.

The giraffes have grown wiser
And they now teach their young
There's a way to outsmart the
tree's ploy.
Simply travel upwind
Where the smell has not been
For the tastiest leaves to enjoy.

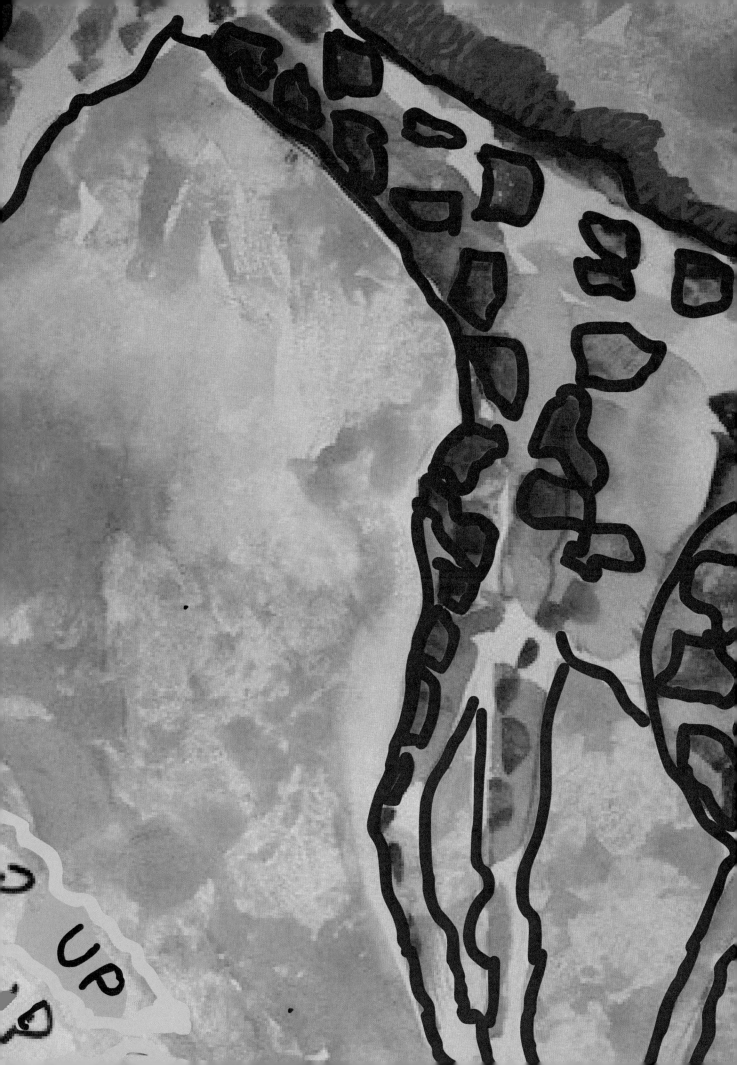

Yes, giraffes taught us first
And we've learned from their work
To explore how trees
Talk to each other.

For deep underground,
Tree's "cell phones" abound
And their root structures
signal each other.

There's a word for this web,
It's called the Wood Wide Web.
When trees talk,
They increase their lifespan.

Some trees grow alone,
Some prefer a dense home.
They live longer
When in groups they stand.

Trees talk through root cells.
They can touch and can tell
If another tree's part of their species.

When they find they're the same
They'll grow close and exchange
Their water and sugar as "freebies".

Momma trees share their meals
Oozing sap through the fields.
Younger trees soak it up and expand.

Grandma trees shield their teens
From the strong, hot sunbeams
Or they'll grow way too slender
than planned.

Older trees in the forest
That are doomed to their death
Send their left-over strength
to the earth.

Then the forest survives
With the food this provides
So young saplings can widen their girth.

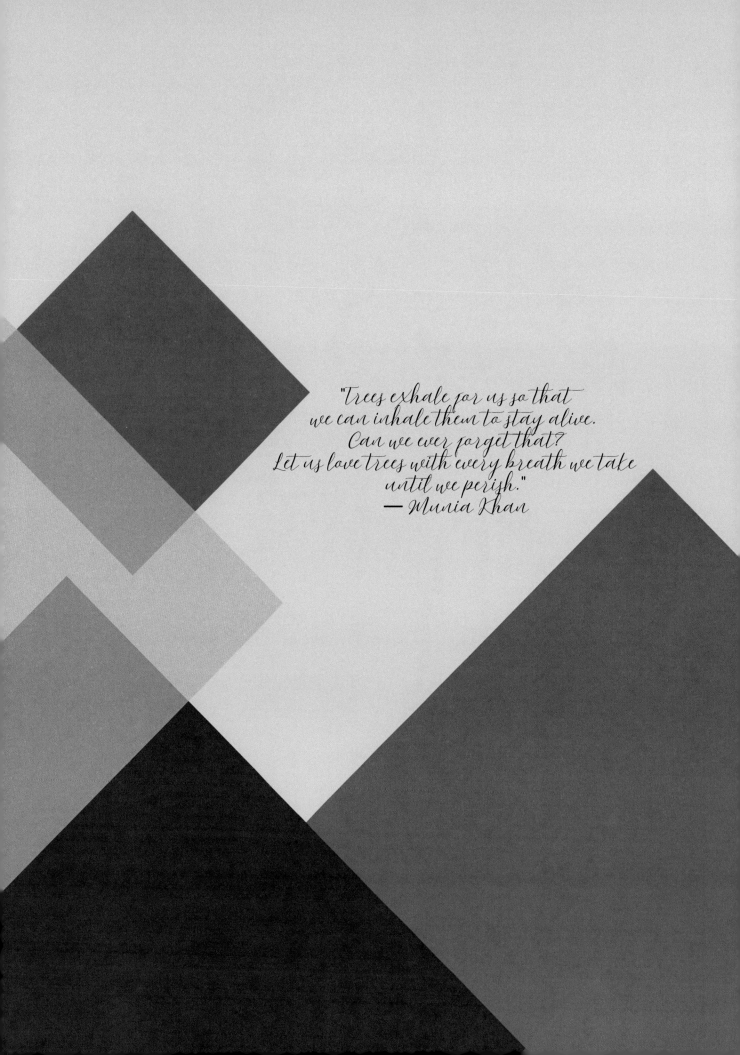

"Trees exhale for us so that
we can inhale them to stay alive.
Can we ever forget that?
Let us love trees with every breath we take
until we perish."
— Munia Khan

Often trees are good friends
So they like to hold hands,
Intertwining their roots
underground.

If their friends should get sick
They will nurture them quick
And protect them from dangers at hand.

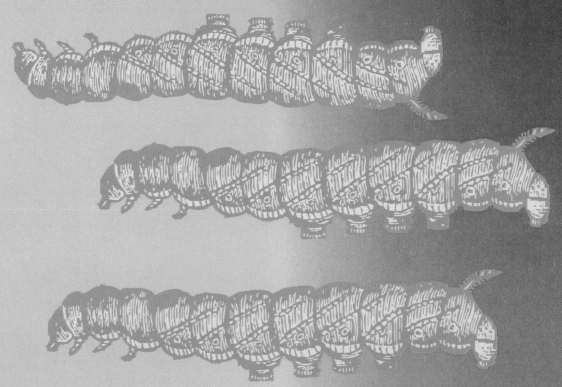

Trees have animal friends
On their help they depend
To protect trees from insect attacks.

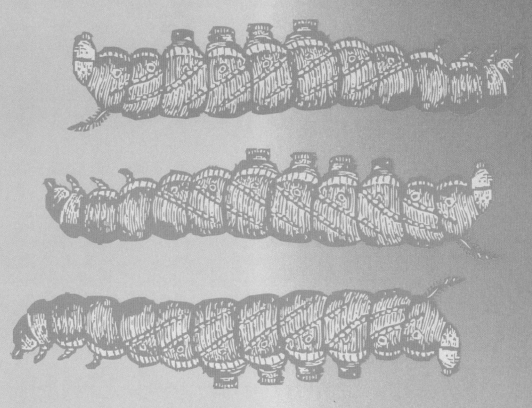

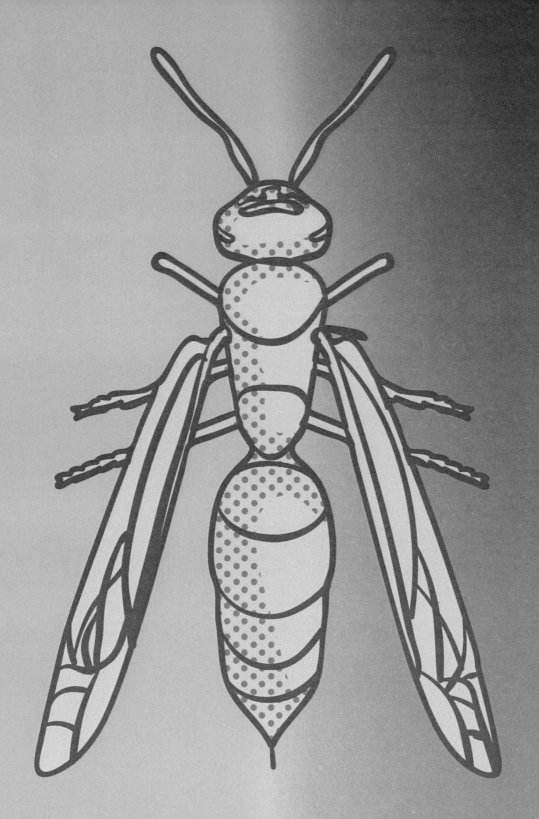

When a caterpillar bites
An elm tree will invite
Rival wasps who will quickly
fight back.

Trees have weapons, too,
Which they are able to use
When another tree inches too near.

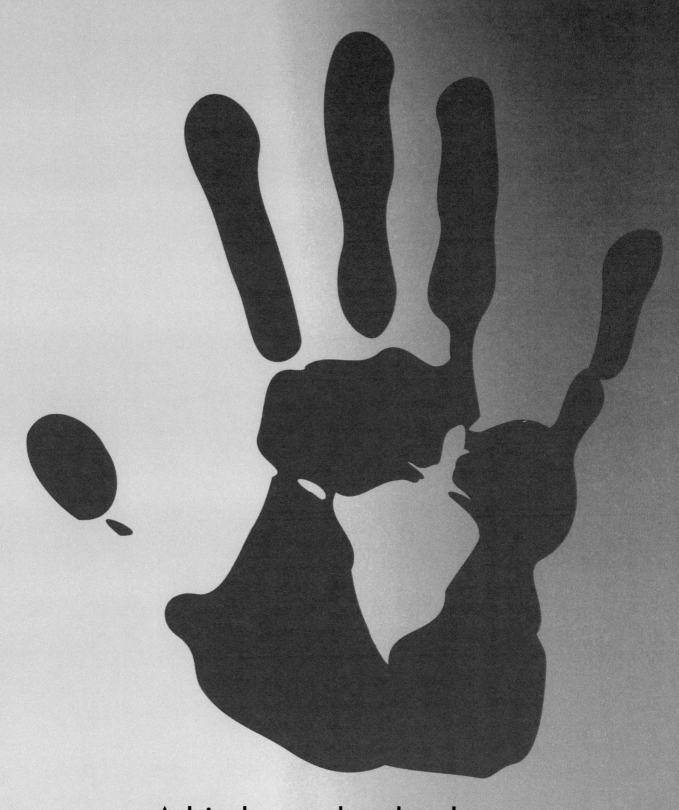

A birch tree has knobs
That feel like sandpaper swabs
Telling neighbors,
"Move back and stay clear."

At night when you sleep
Trees' limbs and leaves weep
Which suggest that at night the trees doze.

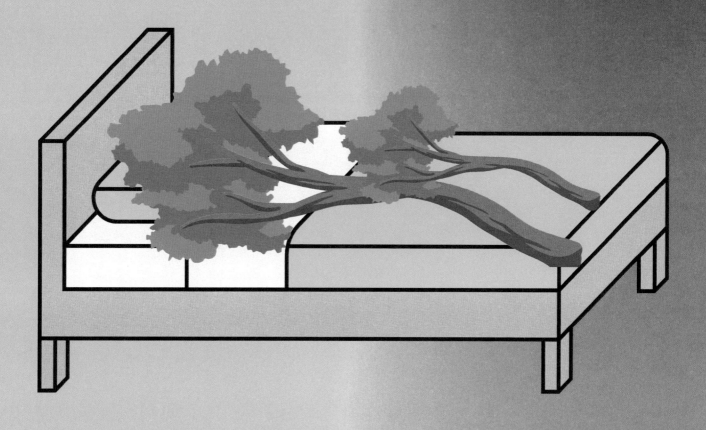

Leaves don't make their food
When the light is subdued.
So, like us,
They relax and repose.

Trees are bound to amaze
As we learn from their ways
That our Earth is
Quite keenly connected.

With this lesson in mind
We must work 'til we find
How to care for our Earth
'Til perfected!

Trees

REFERENCES

Wohllenben, P. (2019) Can you hear the trees talking? Greystone Kids.
Kelley, T. (2022) Listen to the language of the trees: A story of how forests communicate underground (M.Hermansson, Illus.). Dawn Publications.

TYPES OF TREES

Evergreen

Do not lose their leaves all at once and stay green year round.

Deciduous

Leaves change colour in Autumn, before falling to the ground.

STRUCTURE

Crown of foliage

Twigs

Branches

Trunk

Roots

TREE USES

- Produce oxygen and clean the air
- Shade
- Shelter
- Animal homes
- Fuel for heating
- Timber for construction
- Source of food - seeds, nuts, fruit, bark, flowers, sap and pollen

LIFECYCLE

Seed ➡ Sprout ➡ Seedling ➡ Sapling ➡ Mature tree

How to Save Trees

1. Use less paper.

2. Buy recycled paper products.

3. Go for cloth products over paper when possible.

4. Look for volunteer opportunities to protect trees.

5. Spread the word about trees on social media.

6. Stay on the footpaths and trails.

7. Leave dead trees standing.

8. Plant trees.

Life Cycle of a TREE

Name _____

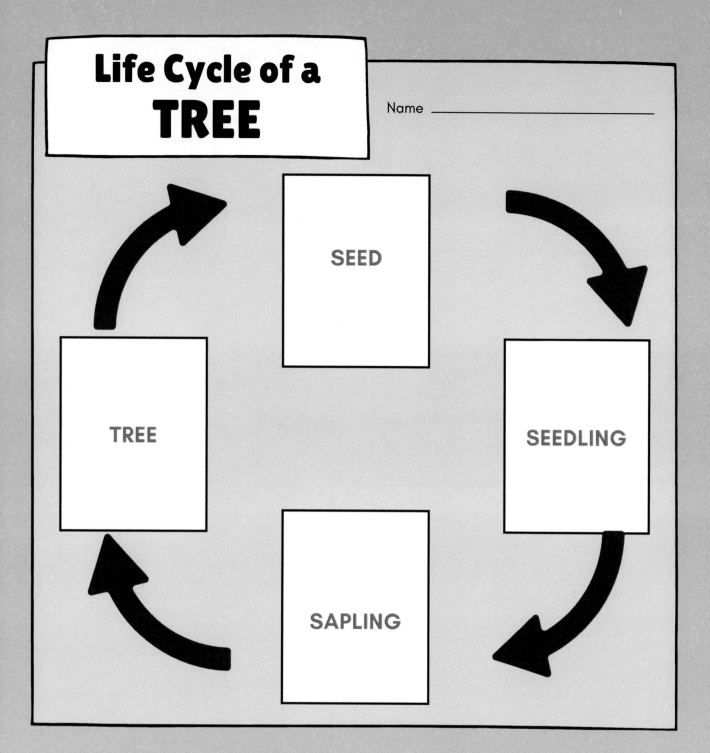

SEED

SEEDLING

SAPLING

TREE

Cut around the images and place in order on the lifecycle diagram above

THe Super Power of Plants

The Photosynthesis Process

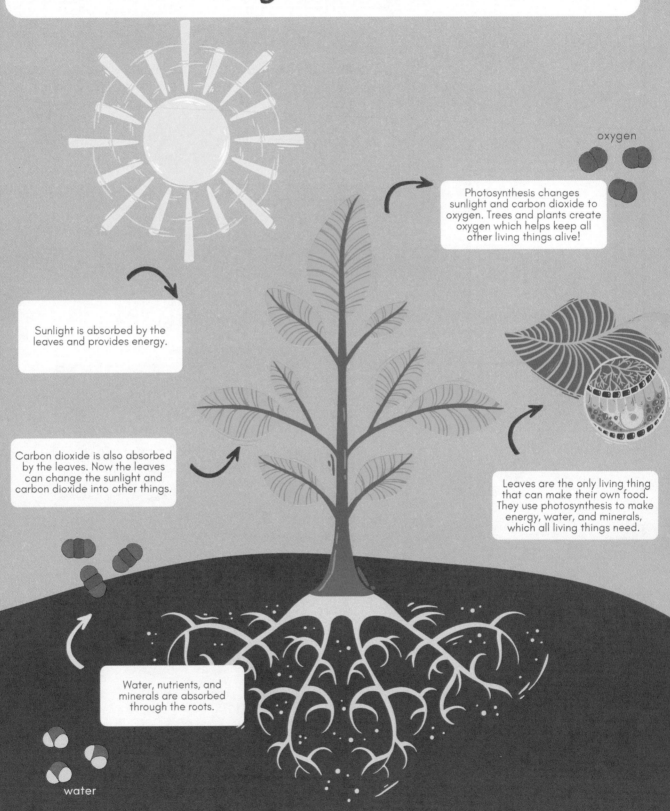

oxygen

Photosynthesis changes sunlight and carbon dioxide to oxygen. Trees and plants create oxygen which helps keep all other living things alive!

Sunlight is absorbed by the leaves and provides energy.

Carbon dioxide is also absorbed by the leaves. Now the leaves can change the sunlight and carbon dioxide into other things.

Leaves are the only living thing that can make their own food. They use photosynthesis to make energy, water, and minerals, which all living things need.

Water, nutrients, and minerals are absorbed through the roots.

water

BENEFiTS OF TREES FOR OUR EARTH

Creating Oxygen

- Trees absorb carbon dioxide and release oxygen through the process of photosynthesis.
- One mature tree can produce enough oxygen for two people every year.

Reducing Air Pollution

- Trees filter air pollutants such as dust, smoke and dangerous chemicals.
- Tree leaves trap pollution particles, helping to maintain better air quality.

Preventing Soil Erosion

- Tree roots bind soil particles together, preventing erosion caused by wind and water.
- By preventing erosion, trees help maintain healthy soil.

Providing Habitats for Wildlife

- Trees are home to various species of birds, insects and other animals.
- By providing shelter and a food source, trees support biodiversity.

Lowering Air Temperature

- Trees provide a cooling effect through shade and water evaporation from the leaves.
- Green areas with lots of trees can reduce urban air temperatures by several degrees.

CLIMATE CHANGE

AND WILDLIFE

HABITAT LOSS

Climate change is altering habitats, forcing wildlife to migrate or adapt to new conditions. Many species are struggling to survive.

CHANGING MIGRATION PATTERNS

Migratory species, like birds and marine animals, face disrupted routes and timing, affecting their survival and reproduction

THREATENED SPECIES

Iconic species such as polar bears, elephants, and coral reefs are particularly vulnerable to the impacts of climate change.

CONSERVATION EFFORTS

Support wildlife conservation programs, protect natural habitats, and reduce your carbon footprint to help safeguard our planet's biodiversity.

Name:_____   **Date:**_____

TREE LEAVES

Please draw a line from the leaf to the correct name.

WILLOW
BIRCH
MAPLE
OAK
ELM
PINE

PLANT A TREE

Enjoy clean air as you watch it grow. Observe the wildlife that will visit your trees.

GROW A FUTURE

PLANT TREES

Plant a tree in your community today!

Find a tree that doesn't have a pair

FUN FACTS ABOUT TREES

Did you know?

WATER

1

Trees are like sponges. They soak up our water and filter it to make it cleaner. Then it flows back into our rivers and streams.

OLD AGE

2

Trees deteriorate but for a long time they never die. Some trees in California are 500 years old.

DIRECTIONS

3

Trees can point to the right direction. Moss grows on the north side of the tree in the Northern Hemisphere and the south side of the tree in the Southern hemisphere.

TYPES

4

There are over 60,000 species of trees, but most of them are from just 10 families.

SPACE

5

Some trees have been to outer space. The Apollo 14 space mission took trees to the moon and found that they grow just like they do on earth.

SEEDS

6

A large oak tree can drop 10,000 acorns in one year. The squirrels are very happy about that!

Leaf Sudoku

Can you tell what type of leaf is missing in each square. Remember, all the leaves in each line, whether horizontal or vertical must be different.

Learn character from trees,
values from roots,
and change from leaves.

— Tasneern Harneed

My Family Tree

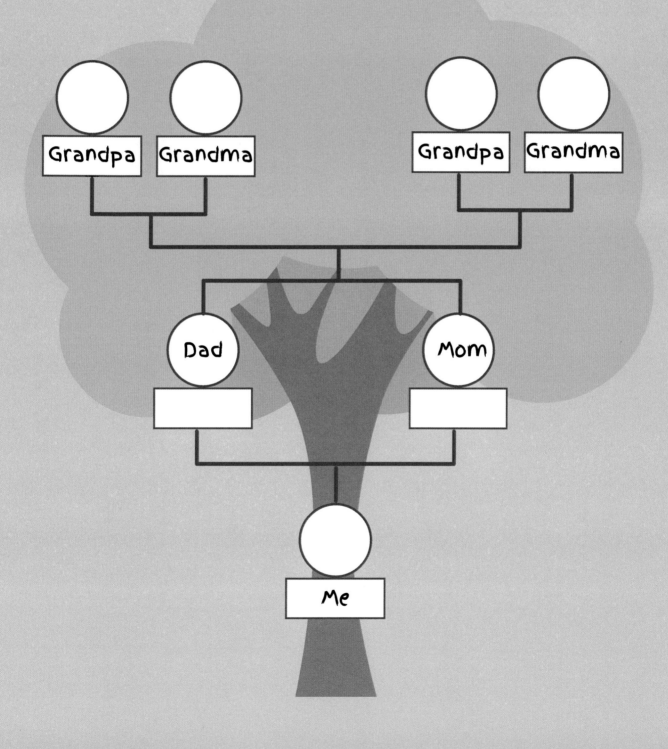